This book was written after asked me how they explai they have to go and see a doctor but that they are not unwell.

Through my experience it is always best to be honest with your child. If they know what to expect then there are no surprises that can cause upset at the time or later!

I am able to confidently write this book after raising my own four children and two step children with four of them also being on the Autistic Spectrum and various other co-occurring conditions. I have studied hard and earnt a BSc in Psychology, an MSc in Clinical and Developmental Neuropsychology, in addition to receiving training for Carol Grays Social Stories^{TM}.

I am learning about going to the Doctors

Doctors are people that have learnt how different parts of the body work

Doctors sometimes work in buildings that look like a house.
This is called a Clinic.

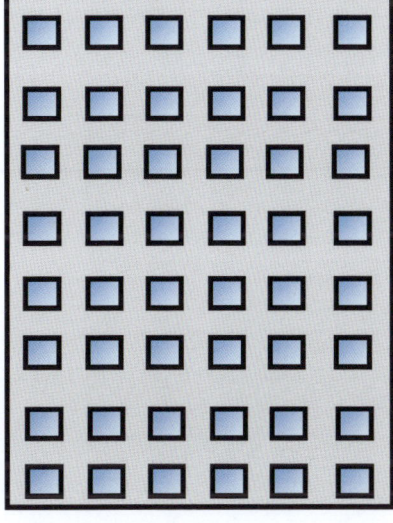

And sometimes Doctors work in a big building called a Hospital

Usually, people go to the Doctor's because they feel poorly

Or

Because they have hurt themselves

Sometimes they go to the Doctor's to see if a part of their body is working differently to other peoples body

This is Okay!

Some Doctors listen to your heart

This is okay

Some Doctors use a needle to take some blood

This is okay

I am going to see a Doctor that is just going to talk

This is okay

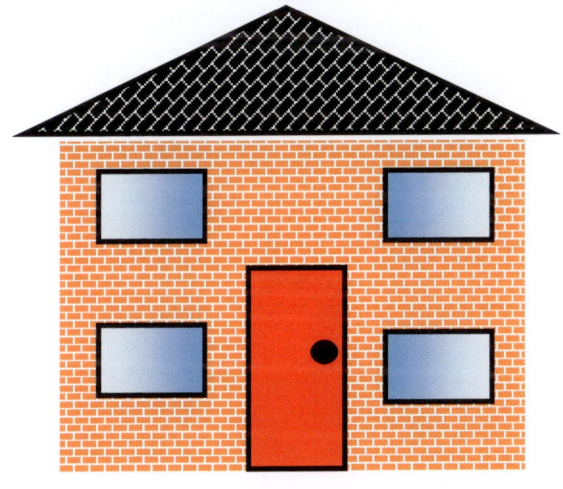

I am going to a Clinic.
It might look a bit like this building

There will be two Doctor's at my appointment and both will say hello and talk to me and my adults for a short time.

Then my adults will go with one doctor who will ask questions about me when I was younger and what I like now

I will go with the other doctor who will ask me some questions about what I like to do and what makes me sad.

We will also play some games

This is okay!
I will go back to my adults soon

This is to see if my brain works differently to other people's.

This is okay

Everyone has something different

Some people can do
some things, and
others are still
learning,
like riding a bike

Other people
can do other
things very
quickly, like
finish a puzzle

We are all different.

That is okay

Questions you may want to ask the Doctor

_____

_____

_____

_____

_____

_____

_____

Questions you may want to ask the Doctor

_____

_____

_____

_____

_____

_____

_____

Ask an Adult to help with the dates of the month and circle when your appointment is.

You can then count down to the date that you are going to see the Doctor.

Cross off the days until your Doctors appointment						
Monday	Tuesday	Wednesday	Thursday	Friday	Saturday	Sunday